UNDERSTANDING THE MYSTERIES OF THE CATHOLIC MASS

By

Denis Tufour, LL.M

Contents

Contents

About the Author 4
ACKNOWLEDGEMENT 5
INTRODUCTION 6
THE GREETING 17
THE ACT OF PENITENCE 19
THE GLORY TO GOD 21
THE COLLECT (OPENING PRAYER) 24
THE LITURGY OF THE WORD 25
SILENCE AND THE LITURGY OF THE WORD 26
THE RESPONSORIAL PSALM 28
THE SECOND READING 29
THE PRAYERS OF THE FAITHFUL 33
THE PREPARATION OF THE GIFTS: THE LITURGY OF THE EUCHARIST 35
THE COLLECTION/ OFFERTORY 36
PREPARATION OF THE GIFTS: PREPARATIONS 38
THE EUCHARISTIC PRAYER 43
THE LIFTING UP OF THE BODY OF CHRIST 47
THE LORD'S PRAYER 50
THE RITE OF PEACE 51
INVITATION 53
RECEIVING THE HOLY COMMUNION AND THE PRECIOUS BLOOD 55
THE CONCLUDING RITES 56
THE LITURGICAL POSTURES 58

BIBLE REFERENCES FOR THE CATHOLIC MASS 60

ABOUT THE AUTHOR

Denis Tufour is a Law Tutor and Director of DC Legal Services Ltd. As a Law Practitioner and a Business minded person, Denis has been involved in teaching catechism both in Ghana and the UK.

He attended St Hubert Minor Seminary in Ghana, where he developed his understanding and knowledge about the Catholic Faith. He is a big advocate of the Catholic Faith and has a mission to create awareness of the Catholic Faith and to draw people to God.

ACKNOWLEDGEMENT

The Author extends his thanks to Almighty God for the wisdom and the strength given to him to write this book. He also thanks Mrs. Cecilia Nthabiseng Tufour, LL.M, his Beloved Wife, Mr. Alexander Oppong- Nkrumah, (MA) Communications Studies and Social Entrepreneur, Rev. Fr. Michael Branch, and Fr Cecilia Louis Adu-Poku for their detailed review and suggestions of the content and may God richly bless them.

INTRODUCTION

Nowadays, going to church has become a fashion for most people. People go to church late and they have even forgotten that the church is the House of the Lord as it is written in Luke 19:46 that the Lord's house is a house of prayer.

Church-going has now become institutionalised and hence there is lack of reverence and the desire to glorify the Lord. People do not even bow or genuflect when they enter the church. They do not even understand why they are in the church and they do not know what happens during the mass celebration.

I used to be one when I was growing up. Going to church

was just a routine. I did not have any understanding of the mass and I did not know that through the mass participation I could have a good relationship with Christ.

It was not until I went to the minor seminary, that I understood the real meaning of the catholic mass.

Mass is the name by which the Sacrament of the Eucharist is commonly called in the Catholic church. It is the central act of divine worship which is described as the source and summit of the Christian life. In formal contexts, it is sometimes called the Holy Sacrifice of the Mass.

The Holy Eucharist is the Sacrament in which Jesus Christ gives his Body and Blood to us so that we too can give ourselves to Him in love and be united with Him in Holy Communion. In this way, we are joined with the one Body of Christ which is the Church.

When we eat the Bread, we unite ourselves with the love of Jesus Christ, who gave his Body for us on the cross and the same way when we drink from the chalice, we unite ourselves with Him who even poured out his Blood out of love for us.

We are reminded that Jesus Christ Himself celebrated the Last Supper with His disciples and therein anticipated His death. He gave Himself to His disciples under the signs of bread and wine and commanded them from then on, even after His death to celebrate the Eucharist *(1 Corinthians 11:24)*.

The Mass is mostly celebrated in the church. Whenever we come to church, we should always be glad because we are coming to the Lord's house, the place where people come to give thanks to God according to His command, to receive His blessings and to be healed by His stripes *(Isaiah 53:4-5)*.

The Lord Himself bore our sins in His body on the cross, so that we might die to sins and live for righteousness for by His wounds we have been healed *(1 Peter 2:24)*.

We come to Mass, we remember the sacrifice that Christ did for us, the sacrificial death on the cross so that we can live with Him forever whether alive or dead when He returns *(1 Thessalonians 5:10)*. For that reason, while we were still weak, Christ died for us sinners at the right time *(Romans 5:6)*.

To judge the quality of the Christian life of a community is always a difficult task. There are so many factors that should be considered and the most important of them are hidden.

Nevertheless, if the Holy Mass is the central act of our Catholic life, then Mass- going must surely remain one of the most indicative of these factors. With good reason, therefore we consider the number of people coming to Mass, not only on Sundays but also on weekdays.

A man who fails to love the Mass fails to love Christ. To love the Mass is a guarantee for salvation. But to love the Mass does not mean just being present and no more. It means to be present with faith and devotion. It means to take part in the Mass, realising what it is the Sacrifice of the Cross renewed on the altar and that when we go to Mass, we go, as it were to Calvary.

We should be present in the church like our Blessed Lady standing beside the Cross, in loving contemplation of Christ who offers himself lovingly for each one of us.

This book is therefore designed to create awareness of the Catholic Mass celebration, what happened at the Mass celebration and how to get engaged during the celebration.

For I was glad when they said to me, "let us go to the Lord's house and now we are here, standing inside the gates of Jerusalem. Jerusalem is a city restored in beautiful order and harmony and this is where the tribes come, the tribes of Israel to give thanks to the Lord" *(Psalm 122:1-4).*

THE ORDER OF THE MASS THE ENTRANCE PROCESSION

Sing to the LORD, all the world! Worship the LORD with joy; come before him with happy songs. Acknowledge that the LORD is God. He made us, and we belong to him; we are his people, we are his flock. Enter the Temple gates with thanksgiving; go into its courts with praise. Give thanks to him and praise him.

The LORD is good; His love is eternal and His faithfulness lasts forever! (Psalm100:1-5).

The Mass begins when the people start to gather for worship. This is the visible beginning of the Mass which starts with the entrance procession of the priest and other ministers taking part in the Mass with an entrance song.

This is the time we are reminded to make a joyful noise to the Lord, to serve the Lord with gladness, to come before His presence with singing and dancing.

This is to know that the Lord is God and it is He who has made us and not ourselves, for we are His people and the sheep of His pasture *(Psalm 100:3)*.

We should therefore bear in mind that we enter the Lord's gates with thanksgiving, His courts with praise and to be thankful to Him; to bless His name, for the Lord is good, His mercy is everlasting and His truth endures to all generation *(Psalm 100:1-5)*.

In 2 Samuel 6:12-15, we learnt that when King David was told that the Lord has blessed the household of Obed-Edom and everything he has because of the ark of God, David went to bring up the ark of God from the house of Obed-Edom to the City of David with rejoicing. When those who were carrying the ark of the Lord had taken six steps, David sacrificed a bull and a fattened calf. Wearing a linen ephod, David danced before the Lord with all his might while he and all Israel were bringing up the ark of the Lord with shouts and the sound of trumpets.

This is the case in our lives these days. Looking at all the blessings God has bestowed on us, we are therefore reminded to enter His gates with praise and dancing, to pour our gratitude to Him and to sing His praise throughout the world.

The entrance song unites the people in a community of worship and introduces the people to the celebration of the day and with a joyful heart, we give ourselves to God.

When we sing praises to God, we magnify our Creator and we adore Him.

When we sing, we obey God. In Colossians 3:16, we are told to let the word of Christ dwell in us richly, to teach and to admonish one another in all wisdom, to sing psalms and hymns and spiritual songs, with thankfulness in our hearts to God. We sing to the Lord as long as we live and shout for joy for the Lord has done it.

During the Lenten season, we are reminded in Joel 2:12-13 to repent sincerely, to return to God with fasting, weeping and mourning, to let our broken heart show our sorrow as tearing our clothes is not enough and to come back to the LORD our God. For the Lord is kind and full of mercy; He is patient and keeps his promise; He is always ready to forgive and not to punish. Therefore, we expect the songs this time will be sorrowful.

As the procession reaches the altar, the priest kisses the altar, in effect, greeting Christ.

The altar stone signifies Christ as the cornerstone of that building which is the Church, the People of God, His body, just as God revealed in 1 Peter 2:6 that: "Behold, I am laying a stone in Zion, a cornerstone, chosen and precious, and whoever believes in it shall not be put to shame."

Jesus is the perfect foundation stone God has chosen for the house. Those who trust in Him are also living stones used to build the house.

In addition, we individually serve as both the priests and the spiritual sacrifices, our lives offered to the builder. Thus, we must live good lives, as strangers in the world preparing to go home to be with our Father, engaged in battle against our desire to sin.

Jesus tells us that He will never forsake us or abandon us and He will not leave us orphans; He will come to us and He is with us always, until the end of the age *(John 14:18)*.

Jesus comes to us in the Mass. Jesus is present with us in the mass; for He said, where two or three are gathered in my name, there am I in their midst *(Matthew 18:20)*. Therefore, once we are inside the church, we all need to give an absolute reverence to Christ.

THE SIGN OF THE CROSS

Therefore, go and make disciples of all nations, baptising them in the name of the Father and of the Son and of the Holy Spirit (Matthew28:19).

The priest now invites the people to beginning the mass celebration in the name of the Father, the Son and the Holy Spirit.

This is to affirm our faith in the Blessed Trinity by beginning our prayer to the Father through the Son in the Holy Spirit. As we pray through the Blessed Trinity, we received a blessing and we invoke the blessing of God as we demonstrate with a visible sign that we belong to Christ. The prayer is both spoken and gestured, and both must be done with reverence and respect.

It should be borne in mind that the sign of the cross is a potent prayer that engages the Holy Spirit as the divine advocate and agent of our successful Christian living.

It also prepares us for receiving God's blessing and disposes us to cooperate with His grace and sanctifies our day.

In moving our hands from our foreheads to our hearts and then both shoulders, we are asking God's blessing for our mind, our passions and desires, our very bodies. In other words, the Sign of the Cross commits us, body and soul, mind and heart, to Christ.

In lifting our hand to our forehead, we recall that the Father is the first person of the Trinity. In lowering our hand, we express that the Son proceeds from the Father and in ending with the Holy Spirit, we signify that the Spirit proceeds from both the Father and the Son.

We also crucify ourselves with Christ by making the sign of the cross. Whoever wishes to follow Christ must deny himself and take up his cross as Jesus told the disciples in Matthew 16:24.

The Sign of the Cross recalls the forgiveness of sins and the reversal of the Fall by passing from the left side of the curse to the right of blessing.

The movement from left to right also signifies our future

passage from present misery to future glory just as Christ crossed over from death to life and from Hades to Paradise.

So therefore, as Christians and Catholics, since we make the sign of the cross many times during the day, we must never become complacent in how we make the sign of the cross. We are praying, not shooing flies.

THE GREETING

For you know the grace of our Lord Jesus Christ, that though He was rich, yet for your sakes He became poor, so that you through His poverty might become rich (2 Corinthians 8:9).

After the sign of the cross, the priest greets the people saying: "The Lord be with you," to which the people respond, "And with your spirit."

This greeting is a shortened version of the greeting given by Paul in 2 Corinthians 13:14 "the grace of our Lord Jesus Christ and the love of God and the fellowship of the Holy Spirit be with you all".

"The Lord be with you" is used at Mass at certain important moments during the celebration.

It helps us to focus when prayer, a reading or an action is about to happen.

It is a greeting that helps us focusing our beginning something.

Above all it is about the presence of Jesus Christ and occurs at four important moments during the Mass celebration to help us think about the presence of our Lord Jesus Christ.

Through this greeting we recognise Christ's presence in the priest and in the gathered assembly, and our faith in the Holy Trinity.

This greeting is found many times in the Bible. It is used to promise that God shall be with someone (Amos 5:14) or a prayer that God will protect or help (Joshua 14:12).

It can be used to say hello or goodbye (Ruth 2:4 1 Samuel 17:37, 20:13) and in Latin to mean in both a prayer that God should be with someone or a confident statement that God is present among them.

At the beginning of Mass, we remember that we gather in the presence of Christ for where two or three are gathered together in my name' Matt 18:20).

At the proclamation of the Readings, we remember Christ speaks to us in the Word and at the beginning of the Eucharistic Prayer, when Christ becomes present among us as we share in his sacrifice under sacramental signs and at the end of Mass, Christ is with us as we glorify him by our lives and witness.

THE ACT OF PENITENCE

Be merciful to me, O God, because of your constant love. Because of your great mercy wipe away my sins. Wash away all my evil and make me clean from my sin. I recognise my faults; I am always conscious of my sins. I have sinned against you, only against you and done what you consider evil. So, you are right in judging me; you are justified in condemning me (Psalm 51:1-4)

To come to God on the altar, we must wash our hands in innocence *(Psalm 26:6)*. If we say we have no sin, we deceive ourselves and the truth is not with us *(1 John 1:8)*.

When we confess our sins, the Lord is faithful and just to forgive us and to cleanse us from all unrighteousness *(1 john 1:9)* and we are called to be holy for the Lord is holy *(1 Peter*

1:16).

We take part in this Act of Penitence, not out of guilt, but out of the loving mercy of the Lord. We call to mind our sins because we are confident in His love and mercy.

We are therefore reminded in James 5:16 that we should confess our sins to each other and pray for each other so that we may be healed.

The prayer of a righteous person is powerful and effective.

After a short period of silence, we express sorrow for our sins, not just in action, but in thought, word, and in failing to act.

We then ask pardon from God by asking His Saints, and our fellow brothers and sisters to also intercede and plead for clemency for us.

THE GLORY TO GOD

"Sing for joy you heavens, for the Lord has done this; shout aloud, you earth beneath. Burst into song you mountains, you forest and all your trees, for the LORD has redeemed Jacob, he displays his glory in Israel" (Isaiah 44:23).

This is the song of angels. It was first sung at the birth of Christ Luke 2:14-15 when they went to announce the good-news of Jesus birth to the shepherds.

The place of this song in the Mass conveys a similar message that is, the good-news that the sins we confessed have been forgiven and as such we can approach God in the Opening prayer.

We recognise the goodness and mercy of the Lord God

through his Son, Jesus Christ by praising the Lord, echoing the angels at the birth of our Lord Jesus Christ:"glory to God in the highest, and on earth peace to men of good will" *(Luke 2:14)* , by singing to the Lord a new song and singing His praise from the end of the earth *(Isiah 42:10)*.

We are to sing the glory of the name of the Lord, to make His praise glorious *(Psalm 66:2) and a*s a manifestation of His work , all creation brings glory to Him.

In Genesis 1:31 we read that God saw all that he had made was very good and for that reason the heavens are declaring the glory of God, the skies are proclaiming the work of his hands*(Psalm 19:1),* and so therefore, God's very work praises Him and brings Him glory. We are to sing glory to God in all our might and strength. Our understanding cannot comprehend God's mighty actions and the beauty of all His creations.

Glory to God is displayed through His mighty actions. In Psalm 111:3, it is said that glorious and majestic are His deeds, and His righteousness endures forever and for that reason we sing of the ways of the Lord, for the glory of the Lord is great(*Psalm 138:5).*

In Exodus 15:11, we are reminded that , "who among the

gods is like You, O Lord? Who is like You, majestic in holiness, awesome in glory, working wonders? No one can accomplish what God can. He is above and beyond our comprehension". So therefore, bringing glory to God is the life purpose of Jesus Christ.

Following His birth, the angels declared the glory of God and suddenly a great company of the heavenly host appeared with the angel, praising God.

Glorifying God the Father was Jesus' role on earth. In John 8:54, Jesus said: "if I glorify myself, my glory means nothing. My Father, whom you claim as your God, is the one who glorifies me".

Glory to God is expressed by John as he describes the eternal heaven. Revelation 21:23 says that the city does not need the sun or the moon to shine on it, for the glory of God gives it light, and the Lamb is its lamp.

By giving God praise and adoration, we are expressing our gratitude for what God has given us *(Philippians 4:11)*.

We are called to be selfless and humble *(Philippians 2:3-4)*. We show love, joy, peace, patience, kindness, goodness, faithfulness, gentleness, and self-control in our lives *(Galatians 5:22-23)*.

This is because we recognise that nothing we have is ours

apart from the will of God. All our talents, abilities, even our possessions, are for God because God has allowed them into our life.

THE COLLECT (OPENING PRAYER)

For our transgressions are multiplied before You, and our sins testify against us; For our transgressions are with us, and we know our iniquities (Isaiah 59:12).

Here the priest celebrant representing Christ, invites the congregation to pray. He "collects" each single prayer, mental as well as vocal and raises them to God as he (celebrant) sums it up with the prayer in the Roman Missal.

This is an important reminder that the celebrant invites us to pray, so everyone in the church must pray during this time.

We then acknowledge our mutual sinfulness and need for mercy, and give praise to God for His goodness and glory to all of us.

This prayer takes all of our individual needs and focuses them, collects them into a common purpose for celebrating the Mass of the day.

THE LITURGY OF THE WORD

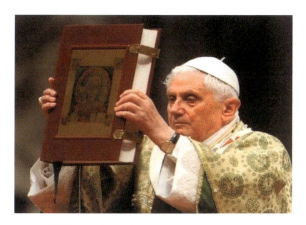

And He said to them, go into all the world, and preach the gospel to every creature (Mark 16:15)

After the collect is finished and everyone sits down, the Mass continues with the Liturgy of the Word. The Liturgy of the Word is comprised of scripture readings, a homily, the profession of faith, and the prayers of the faithful.

The structure of readings consists of a first reading, a responsorial psalm, a second reading, a Gospel acclamation, and a Gospel.

We must prepare ourselves interiorly for the great thing that is about to take place as Christ is present. During Jesus's lifetime, multitudes of people flocked to him, because they were seeking his healing presence.

SILENCE AND THE LITURGY OF THE WORD

As Jesus and his disciples were on their way, he came to a village where a woman named Martha opened her home to him. She had a sister called Mary, who sat at the Lord's feet listening to what he said. But Martha was distracted by all the preparations that had to be made. She came to him and asked, "Lord, don't you care that my sister has left me to do the work by myself? Tell her to help me!" Martha, Martha," the Lord answered, "you are worried and upset about many things but few things are needed or indeed only one. Mary has chosen what is better, and it will not be taken away from her"(Luke 10:38-42).

The structure of the Liturgy of the Word lends itself not just to hearing the Word of God, but to listening. To listen, we need an active, engaged mind that is focused on the Word of God, and we need time to process what we have heard for meaning.

For this reason, it's important to make good use of the

silences in between the readings. If we take time throughout the Liturgy of the Word to reflect, we are more open to that Word as we listen to the Gospel and the homily.

THE FIRST READING

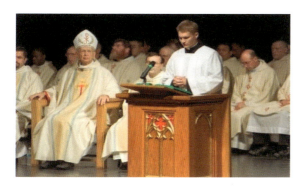

The first reading is generally taken from the Old Testament, with two exceptions: during the Easter season, the first reading will come from the book of Acts, as it narrates into details the beginning of the Church and on certain solemnities (All Saints and Immaculate Conception), the first reading will come from the book of Revelation.

The first reading is always linked in some way to the Gospel, more than any of the other readings proclaimed at Mass. The first reading highlights the Gospel in one of many ways:

- To show how a prophecy in the Old Testament is fulfilled through Jesus Christ in the Gospel

- To make a contrast between events and personalities in the Old Testament and the Gospel
- To make the meaning of the Gospel clearer

THE RESPONSORIAL PSALM

Following the first reading, there is a period of silence to reflect on what has been proclaimed.

This silence helps us to better understand the reading.

When we use the silence for this purpose, we participate more completely in the Liturgy of the Word. After this period of silence, we raise our voices in song through the Responsorial Psalm and through our participation in the sung antiphon, as well as listening to the verses.

THE SECOND READING

The Second Reading is a semi-continuous reading taken from the Letters in the New Testament of the Bible. The Letters in the New Testament are written to the early church by St. Paul and the Apostles. These letters offer support, encouragement, correction, and guidance to us.

We also need the direction of the Apostles, guided by the Holy Spirit, as we make our way through a society that doesn't always support us in living our faith.

The only exception to the semi-continuous second reading is during the seasons of Advent, Lent, and Easter. During these seasons, the readings are selected to highlight the theme of the season.

A second reading during Advent might talk about the need to watch and prepare, while a second reading during Easter might talk about the glory of the Resurrection.

GOSPEL ACCLAMATION

The Gospel Acclamation is a song of praise. We prepare to hear the Gospel of Jesus Christ by singing praise to Him. During most of the year we sing "Alleluia" (Praise to God).

This serves as a bridge linking the readings and the Gospel.

During Lent, another acclamation is substituted, as the Alleluia is seen as too joyful to be sung during the season of Lent. Our participation in the singing of the Gospel Acclamation is very important.

THE GOSPEL

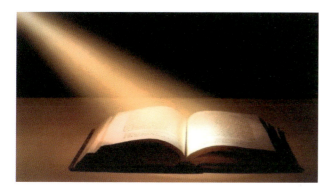

This is the highpoint of the Liturgy of the Word, the Gospel reading. The word Gospel means "good news", the best news we can hear as Jesus Christ speaks to us.

We should pay especially close attention to the words of the Gospel as they are proclaimed.

THE CREED (PROFESSION OF FAITH)

Therefore, holy brothers, who share in the heavenly calling, set your minds on Jesus, the apostle and high priest whom we confess (Hebrews 3:6).

A creed is a statement or summary of belief. The structure of the creed reinforces our belief in the Holy Trinity, first addressing the Father, then the Son, and then the Holy Spirit, stressing that the three persons are one God. At the heart of our faith is our belief that God became one of us at the birth of Christ.

To highlight our belief in this truth, we are asked to bow at the words "by the power of the Holy Spirit, he was born of the Virgin Mary, and became man".

On Easter Sunday or on Sundays when we have baptisms, we are asked to renew our baptismal promises.

We are asked about our belief, to which we respond "I do"

to each statement of our faith. The renewal of our baptismal promises is also a creed, a statement of belief, based on the Apostle's Creed.

The Creed is a statement of the truths which we hold as Catholics. When we pray this prayer together, we express not only our individual belief but the faith which all of us hold in common.

THE PRAYERS OF THE FAITHFUL

With one accord, they all continued in prayer, along with the women and Mary the mother of Jesus, and with His brothers (Acts 1:14)

The Prayers of the Faithful, also known as the General Intercessions or the Universal Prayers, take place at the conclusion of the Liturgy of the Word, and serve like a hinge connecting the Liturgy of the Word to the Liturgy of the Eucharist.

The content of what is prayed after the sermon is taken from the encouragement of Saint Paul in first Timothy, which admonishes Timothy to pray for all people (1 Timothy 2:1-2).

The Church re-echoes this by praying for the intentions of the church and the world at large.

When we pray theses prayers, we offer them for the needs of the Church, for peace, for good harvest, for the country and city, for the sick, the poor and the needy, for those who have died and for forgiveness of sins.

This is the time we pray not just for those needs close to us as individuals, but for the needs of the parish, the diocese, the country and for the Church as a whole.

When we pray in this way, we recognise our place within the larger community of the baptised, and bring those prayers and intentions with us as we move forward in the Mass.

THE PREPARATION OF THE GIFTS: THE LITURGY OF THE EUCHARIST

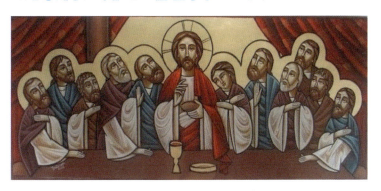

Overview

While they were eating, Jesus took bread, and when he had given thanks, he broke it and gave it to his disciples, saying, "take it; this is my body". Then he took a cup, and when he had given thanks, he gave it to them, and they all drank from it this is my blood of the covenant, which is poured out for many", he said to them truly I tell you, I will not drink again from the fruit of the vine until that day when I drink it new in the kingdom of God (Mark 14:21-25)

In the same way at Mass, Christ, present through the priest, celebrating the Mass, takes bread and wine, gives thanks and says the same words of Christ: "this is my Body… this is my Blood".

As Catholics, we believe that through this action and the action of the Holy Spirit, the bread and wine become the Body and Blood of Christ which we share, just as the disciples did at the Last Supper.

For whenever we eat this bread and drink this cup, we proclaim the Lord's death until he comes in glory.

THE COLLECTION/ OFFERTORY

Each of you should give what you have decided in your heart to give, not reluctantly or under compulsion, for God loves a cheerful giver and God is able to bless you abundantly, so that in all things at all times, having all that you need, you will abound in every good work (2 Corinthians 9:7-8)

After we have sat down following the prayers of the faithful, the collection takes place. The collection is not just a practical need that must take place but a spiritual need.

Here we offer to God a sacrifice of thanksgiving, and perform our vows to the Most High *(Psalm 50:14)*.

We can bring whatever gift we have for the good of the

community. These include bread and wine for the Mass, but other gifts such as animals, eggs, produce, cloth, or whatever is our best gift to offer and the need for the good of people are also acceptable to God.

The monetary gifts we place in the collection represent the gift of our lives, and the gift of living out the faith in the world during the past week.

When we bring forward the collection to the altar, it represents our lives also being united with the altar and what is about to take place.

While the offerings are being taken up, a song is usually sung. This song expresses our joy at what is about to take place in the Mass, and often will further reflect on the Gospel of the day.

PREPARATION OF THE GIFTS: PREPARATIONS

Come to me, all you who are weary and burdened, and I will give you rest. Take my yoke upon you and learn from me, for I am gentle and humble in heart, and you will find rest for your souls (Matthew 11:28-29).

During the preparation of the gifts, while the priest gives thanks to God for the gifts of the bread and the wine, we on the other hand, we offer ourselves and everything we have to Jesus Christ.

We cast our burden, we empty ourselves, our worries, our sorrows, our studies, our needs, our struggles, and our weakness to Christ on the altar for he cares for us *(1 Peter 5:7)*.

When the priest mixes a little bit of water into the wine and says, "by the mystery of this water and wine, may we come to share in the divinity of Christ (wine), who humbled himself to share in our humanity (water)", we pray that just as the water and wine become one, that we also become one with Christ.

The priest first takes the paten with the bread and, with both hands, slightly lifts it up over the altar, while saying the corresponding prayer. He does the same with the wine.

The two almost identical prayers that the priest pronounces out loud or quietly are similar to those that Jesus used in His prayers of blessing, according to the Jewish tradition *(berekah; Lk. 10:21; Jn. 11:41)*.

The priest says the following, first over the bread and then over the wine, as Christ did:

- "Blessed are you, Lord, God of all creation. Through your goodness, we have this bread to offer, which earth has given and human hands have made. It will become for us the bread of life".

- "Blessed are you, Lord, God of all creation. Through your goodness, we have this wine to offer, fruit of the vine and work of human hands. It will become our spiritual drink".
The people respond:

- "Blessed be God forever." *(Rm. 9:5; 2 Cor. 11:31)*

After presenting the bread and wine, the priest bows before the altar and prays quietly: "Lord God, we ask you to receive us and be pleased with the sacrifices we offer you with humble and contrite heart".

In this way, the priest prepares to celebrate the Eucharist "in spirit and in truth", knowing that "a broken and contrite heart, O God, thou wilt not despise." *(Ps. 50)*.

Now is the moment when the offerings, the altar, the celebrant, and the people can be incensed. The priest then washes his hands, thus obtaining his "interior purification." Once at the altar again, he calls all present to prayer: "pray, my brothers and sisters, that my sacrifice and yours may be acceptable to God, the almighty Father" and we respond: "may the Lord accept the sacrifice at your hands for the praise and glory of His name, for our good, and the good of all His Church."

In the second Book of Samuel, a plague befell Israel. The prophet Gad went to the King suggesting that a sacrifice be offered to God in prayer that the plague will pass. David approached Araunah to obtain what is needed for the sacrifice, and he says, may the Lord, your God, accept the sacrifice at your hands.

We call the Mass a "sacrifice" because it is the re-presentation of Christ's perfect self-sacrifice on the Cross.

Bread and wine are sacrificed at Jesus' instruction since He said that these elements would re-present His Body and Blood sacrificed on Good Friday.

We are not re-crucifying Christ, but participating in the original offering of Christ as it is made present anew.

The words, "for the praise and glory of His name" come from Psalm 50 where God says that "those who offer praise as a sacrifice glorify Me".

There is no better way to offer praise to, and declare God's glory than by continuing Christ's sacrifice. We give praise and glory to God and to the Name of Jesus since it is by His death and Resurrection that we make peace with God for all of humanity.

This confirms the witness of the Book of Revelation, wherein the numberless multitude in heaven declare, "salvation comes from our God and from the Lamb; praise and glory, wisdom and thanksgiving, honour, power and might be to our God forever and ever".

Saint Paul describes Christ's sacrifice perfectly in Romans 8:28 by writing, "all things work for good for those who love God, who are called according His purpose".

We show our love for God in offering exactly what His Son offered to Him out of love and this is indeed for our good and the good of all who are called according to His purpose, the holy Church.

Jesus certainly wouldn't have done this if it were not for His love of God and all of us.

We are reminded that just as God ended the plague of Israel because of the sacrifice of David, we pray that, through the sacrifice of Christ, perpetuated by the Church, God will pardon the plague of our sins.

We remind ourselves that everyone at Mass is present to ask that the limitless good of the death and Resurrection of Christ be bestowed on our intention and the Mass is the greatest possible prayer since it is the perfect offering of Christ to the Father.

In the Old Testament, Judas Maccabeus sent an offering to the Temple so that a sacrifice of atonement could be offered for those who had lost their lives.

Maccabees 12 says that in doing this Judas and his soldiers acted in an excellent and noble way because they were expecting the resurrection of the dead and went about achieving it for them through sacrifice.

Having Mass said for any intention is as noble and excellent as the sacrifice arranged by Judas Maccabeus.

The heavens open for us during Mass and bringing an intention to the sacrifice is like looking up and praying that Lord remember anew that He died and rose for our intention as well. Every Mass offered for the intention of anyone or anything receives God's special attention and applies the fruits of Christ's death and Resurrection.

The prayers of the faithful, united to those of Christ, are here lifted to God like the incense *(Ps. 141:2; Rev. 5:8, 8:3-4)*. The faithful present unite themselves to Christ the victim and prepare to offer themselves to God as "a fragrant offering and sacrifice". *(Eph 5:2)*.

THE EUCHARISTIC PRAYER

The crowds that went ahead of him and those that followed shouted, "Hosanna to the Son of David!" "Blessed is he who comes in the name of the Lord!" "Hosanna in the highest heaven" (Matthew 21:9)

The word Eucharist means Thanksgiving, and the Eucharistic prayer is a prayer of thanksgiving and petition to God.

During the Eucharistic prayer, through the action of the Holy Spirit and the words of the priest, the bread and wine become the Body and Blood of Christ.

The Eucharistic prayer begins with a dialogue between the

priest and the people. This is the time we lift our hearts to the Lord and to give thanks to God.

This is the time we are spiritually engaged in the Mass and not just physically present.

This dialogue leads into the preface of the Eucharistic prayer. The preface is said by the priest by himself, but we should listen to this prayer and reflect on God's goodness in our lives.

At the conclusion of the preface, we respond to it by singing or saying Holy, holy, holy is the Lord Almighty, the whole earth is full of his glory *(Isiah 6:3)*.

This response is sung with joy for all the good things God has done for us and continues to do for us.

And He withdrew from them about a stone's throw, and He knelt and began to pray (Luke 22:41)

After the congregation sings the "Holy, Holy" acclamation,

everyone except for the priest, deacon and acolyte kneels, unless prevented from doing so because of a physical handicap or lack of space.

Kneeling is a posture of adoration and deep reverence, and is a physical reminder for our minds to be focused on the action taking place at the altar.

We now enter the most important part of the Mass.

For I received from the Lord what I also passed on to you: that the Lord Jesus, on the night He was betrayed, took bread, and when He had given thanks, He broke it and said, "This is My body, which is for you; do this in remembrance. In *the same way, after supper He took the cup, saying, "This cup is the new covenant in My blood; do this, as often as you drink it, in remembrance of Me" (1Corithians 11:23-25).*

While you stretch out your hand to heal, signs and wonders are performed through the name of your holy servant Jesus (Acts 4:30).

This is not a time for going to the restroom, fumbling with the Missal, or other distractions. Every celebration of the Eucharist is the one supper that Christ celebrated with his disciples and at the same time, the anticipation of the banquet that the Lord will celebrate with us at the end of time.

We should note that is the Lord who calls us to worship God and in mysteries presented in the liturgy.

Continuing the Eucharistic Prayer, the priest will continue his prayer of thanksgiving that was started in the preface. In some Eucharistic prayers, this thanksgiving may only be a sentence, while other Eucharistic Prayers will dive deeply into the life of Jesus.

Regardless of its length, our hearts should be full of gratitude for God's many gifts, especially the gift we are about to receive from the altar.

The priest, who up to this point has held his hands extended upward, an ancient posture for prayers directed to God the Father now extends his hands over the bread and wine, palms down instead of up, asking the Father to send the Holy Spirit upon the gifts of bread and wine and make them holy. This reminds us that when the Lord sends His Spirit.

This part of the Eucharistic Prayer is called the epiclesis. The gesture of laying on hands has been used from the time of the apostles to call down the Holy Spirit. At this point of the Mass the deacon (when physically able) will also kneel, signaling the importance of this point in the liturgy.

THE LIFTING UP OF THE BODY OF CHRIST

And when I am lifted from the earth, I will draw all people to myself (John 12:32)

The priest then moves into the Institution Narrative. The priest recalls the words of Christ at the Last Supper, the first Mass. When the priest takes, the bread lifts it up and says, "This is my Body," the bread has truly become the Body of Jesus Christ.

Now, we are reminded in that "Here Jesus in being lifted and all our eyes must be fixed on Him, the Sovereign Lord because in Him we take refuge and we ask Him not to leave us defenseless *(Psalm 141:8).*

In the same way, the priest takes the wine and says, "This is the cup of my Blood," and the wine truly becomes the Blood of Jesus Christ.

After the consecration of both the bread and wine, the

Body and Blood are elevated for the people to see. The servers ring the bells to signal the people that Someone, important is here. Jesus Christ is with us, Body and Blood, completely and totally in our midst.

Then Jesus said to Thomas, "Put your finger here and look at My hands. Reach out your hand and put it into My side. Stop doubting and believe." Thomas replied, "My Lord and my God!" Jesus said to him, "Because you have seen Me, you have believed; blessed are those who have not seen, and yet have believed(John 20:27- 29)

It is now a great time to adore Christ as He is present in our midst and say silently **"My Lord and My God"** during the elevations.

After the consecration, the priest invites us to "proclaim the Mystery of Faith." We respond by focusing on the saving action of this sacrifice, the sacrifice of His death on the cross and His resurrection.

After the memorial acclamation is sung, the priest continues the Eucharistic Prayer with a remembrance, also called an anamnesis. The priest, on our behalf, recalls the suffering, death, and resurrection of Jesus Christ.

In calling this to mind, we are reminded of Jesus' saving work in the world and of his True Presence in what was consecrated. What we see with our eyes as bread and wine is not a symbol, but the true Body and Blood of Jesus Christ who suffered, died, and was raised from the dead for our redemption.

The priest, again speaking on our behalf, then offers back to the Father the Body and Blood of Jesus Christ on our behalf. As the priest prays out loud, we should listen and pray silently that we too offer our lives, our words and good works with Christ back to the Father.

The priest then petitions the Father on our behalf. He prays for the leaders of the church and all its members, for the peace and salvation of the world, for the needs of those present, and especially for those who have died.

As the priest prays for these needs, we also pray for the needs of those around us, confident that we are united in Christ, praying for and supporting one another.

The Eucharistic prayer concludes with a prayer of praise to God. This prayer reminds us that the entire Eucharistic Prayer has been offered to the Father, through the Son, in the unity of the Holy Spirit.

No words can fully express the joy and excitement we feel at this moment, so we express our acceptance and belief with joy.

After the Eucharistic Prayer is completed, everyone stands. The next series of prayers and actions are designed as one final preparation before we receive the Body and Blood of Christ.

THE LORD'S PRAYER

Do not be like them, for your Father knows what you need before you ask Him. So then, this is how you should pray: 'Our Father in heaven, hallowed be Your name, Your kingdom come, Your will be done, on earth as it is in heaven. Give us this day our daily bread and forgive us our debts, as we also have forgiven our debtors and lead us not into temptation, but deliver us from the evil one (Matthew 6:8-13)

Praying the Our Father together as a community. This prayer is the perfect prayer to say over the Lord's Body and Blood, because it asks for the "Daily Bread" of the Eucharist as well as asking for forgiveness of sins and forgiveness of others.

With these words, God tenderly invites us to believe that He is our true Father and that we are His true children, so that with all boldness and confidence we may ask Him as dear children ask their dear father.

THE RITE OF PEACE

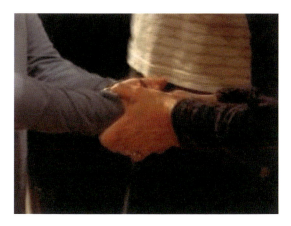

Peace I leave with you; my peace I give you. I do not give to you as the world gives. Do not let your hearts be troubled and do not be afraid (John 14:27. Leave your gift there in front of the altar. First go and be reconciled to them; then come and offer your gift (Matthew 5:24).

The priest then says another prayer, recalling Christ's gift of peace at the Last Supper and our continued prayer for peace and forgiveness of sins.

The priest or deacon then invites us to extend to one another a sign of Christ's peace. The peace that we extend to one another is not an individual wish, but the peace of Jesus Christ.

By extending Christ's peace to one another, we symbolize

our reconciliation with one another before we come forward to receive Communion.

After the sign of peace, the priest will break his Host into smaller pieces for himself and to distribute to the people.

The breaking of the Host reminds us that Christ was broken and died for us, and sharing in the one Host is a reminder that we are united as one Body in Christ, just as Christ did at the Last Supper with His Apostles.

The priest will also take a small piece of the host and place it in the chalice.

Spiritually, mingling the Host with the chalice is a reminder that the Body and Blood of Christ separated in death were brought to life in the Resurrection, and that we receive from the altar the living Body and Blood of Christ.

INVITATION

The next day John saw Jesus coming toward him and said, "Look, the Lamb of God, who takes away the sin of the world. This is He of whom I said, 'A man who comes after me has surpassed me because He was before me (John 1:29-30) and blessed are those who are invited to the marriage supper of the Lamb(Revelation 19:9).

The centurion answered, "Lord, I am not worthy to have You come under my roof. But just say the word, and my servant will be healed. For I myself am a man under authority, with soldiers under me. I tell one to go, and he goes; and another to come, and he comes. I tell my servant to do something, and he does it(Matthew 8:8-9).

While the fraction rite takes place, we sing the "Lamb of God," a beautiful litany that prays once more for God's mercy and peace. During or after the Lamb of God, the priest will say a short prayer asking that he be worthy to receive the Body and Blood of

Christ.

The priest raises the Host and chalice for all to see and says, "This is the Lamb of God, who takes away the sins of the world. Happy are we who have been called to His supper.

We are now filled with joy and anticipation of receiving the Eucharist, but also humility at the incredible gift that we are about to receive by keeping our eyes on Jesus, the champion who initiates and perfects our faith.

Because of the joy awaiting Him, He endured the cross, disregarding its shame. Now He is seated in the place of honor beside God's throne *(Hebrews 12:2)*.

We pray together, "Lord, I am not worthy to receive you, but only say the word and I shall be healed".

We pray with the same humility to be healed and be united with Christ.

RECEIVING THE HOLY COMMUNION AND THE PRECIOUS BLOOD

When we too receive the Body of Christ, the priest or extraordinary minister holds the Communion in front of us and says, "the Body of Christ," to which we respond by bowing our head and saying "Amen."

When we receive from the cup, the deacon, acolyte, or extraordinary minister holds the cup in front of us and says, "the Blood of Christ," to which we respond by bowing our head and saying "Amen."

Receiving the Body and Blood of Christ is a powerful time for us. We sing a communion song, raising our voices in joy and thanksgiving for this gift that we are receiving in the Lord.

We also take time for silence, to listen to Jesus and what He wants from us. We need both the singing and the silence to fully express our love for this gift we have just received from the Father, his Son, our Lord Jesus Christ, now present within us.

AFTER COMMUNION

After communion, the priest, deacon or acolyte will consolidate any remaining Host and place them in the tabernacle.

The Host is placed in the tabernacle for bringing communion to the sick, and for times of private adoration of the Blessed Sacrament whenever the church is open.

The priest then prays the Prayer after Communion. This prayer is not a concluding prayer for the Mass. Instead, it is a prayer on our behalf that the communion we have received bring us spiritual strength and growth in holiness.

THE CONCLUDING RITES

The priest gives us God's blessing before we are dismissed to go in peace to love and serve the Lord. We are also given the graces of God's blessing that we will need as we live out our lives during the week.

The dismissal reminds us that the Mass may be concluded, but our call to live out our Catholic identity goes with us to work, school, our family and friends.

   While we have been dismissed, it is a mark of respect to allow the priest and assisting ministers to leave first.

THE LITURGICAL POSTURES

The liturgical postures of standing, sitting, bowing, kneeling, and prostration are the subject of today's Liturgical Minute.

These postures convey the various relationships that we have with God. Some convey reverence, while others convey repentance, submission, supplication, or adoration. For example, for the first century Christian community, standing was the ordinary posture for prayer, denoting reverence for God and a sign of the resurrection of Christ.

Physical gestures and postures assumed during liturgical worship can express outwardly the inner attitudes of the heart and soul. These gestures and postures do not merely describe inner attitudes, they actually bring such attitudes into existence and manifest the relationship to God that they symbolise.

Today, **standing** continues to be the ordinary posture for prayer.

Sitting is the posture of rest of listening, and to reflect on what has been heard.

A simple bowing of the head is sometimes used for prayer or when receiving a blessing and always before receiving Holy

Communion.

Kneeling can be an expression of humility, of supplication, or a sign of penance or sorrow.

Genuflection, a form of kneeling whereby the right knee touches the ground, is an expression of reverence or a way to show adoration.

As a sign of reverence and adoration, believers genuflect or make a profound bow (being a bow from the waist) when passing close to the Blessed Sacrament reserved in the tabernacle.

A double genuflection, that is, kneeling on both knees and bowing the upper portion of the body slightly and then rising again (or if unable, a profound bow), is a sign of adoration made before the Holy Eucharist exposed.

Prostration, the practice of lying on the ground face downward, a sign of total submission, while practiced often by the early Christians, is now primarily reserved for the rites of ordination.

BIBLE REFERENCES FOR THE CATHOLIC MASS

INTRODUCTORY RITES	Biblical Foundation
WE STAND UP	Mt 28:19
ENTRANCE SONG	I Chron 16:36
	II Cor 13:13
In the name of the Father, and of the Son, and of the Holy Spirit.	
Amen.	
The grace of our Lord Jesus Christ and the love of God and the fellowship of the Holy Spirit be with you all.	
And also with you.	

GLORIA Glory to God in the highest and peace to his people on earth. Lord God, heavenly King, almighty God, and Father, we worship you, we give you thanks, we praise you for your glory. Lord Jesus Christ, only Son of the Father, Lord God, Lamb of God, you take away the sin of the world, have mercy on us; you are seated at the right hand of the Father, receive our prayer. For you alone are the Holy One, you alone are the Lord, you alone are the Most High, Jesus Christ, with the Holy Spirit **in the glory of God, the Father. Amen.**	*GLORIA* Lk. 2:14 Rev 19:6 Rev 22:9; Eph 5:20; Rev 7:2 II Jn 3; Phil 2:11; Jn 1:29 Rom 8:34 Lk 4:34; Lk 1:32 Jn 14:26
each single mass. When he finishes, we answer: **Amen**	

LITURGY OF THE WORD **FIRST READING** The Word of the Lord / **Thanks be to God** **RESPONSORIAL PSALM** **SECOND READING** The Word of the Lord / **Thanks be to God** **ALLELUIA** WE STAND UP The Lord be with you. **And also with you.** A reading from the holy gospel according to... **Glory to you, Lord. (GOSPEL)** This is the gospel of the Lord. **Praise to you, Lord Jesus Christ.** **HOMILY** WE TAKE A SIT WE STAND UP **CREED OR THE PROFESSION OF FAITH** **PRAYER OF THE FAITHFUL OR GENERAL INTERCESSIONS**	Text related to the readings of the Day Old Testament / Acts of the Apostles Psalm New Testament Psalm II Cor 1:2 Gospel- Explanation of Readings Deut 6:4 Gen 14:19 Gen 1:1 Jn 3:16 Acts 2:36 Lk 1:35 Matt 1:22-23 Jn 19:1-2, 17-19 I Pe 3:18-19 I Cor 15:3-4 Mk 16:19 Acts 10:42. II Tim 4:1 Acts 2:17 Rom 5:5 Mt. 16:18. Rom 12:5 Rev 5:1, 7:9, 22:5, 20 Jn 20:23 Rom 8, 11 I Tim 2:1-2

LITURGY OF THE EUCHARIST	Acts 4:35 - II Cor 9:12-13
WE TAKE A SEAT	
PRESENTATION OF GIFTS	Eccl 3:14 Sirach 17
COLLECTION	
Blessed are you, Lord, God of all creation. Through your goodness, we have this bread to offer, which earth has given and human hands have made. It will become for us the bread of life.	Jn 6:35
Blessed be God for ever.	Psm 68, 36
Blessed are you, Lord, God of all creation. Through your goodness, we have this wine to offer, fruit of the vine and work of human hands. I will become our spiritual drink.	Lk 22:17-18 Psm 68:36
Blessed be God for ever.	
Pray, brethren, that our sacrifice may be acceptable to God, the almighty Father.	Heb 12:28
May the Lord accept the sacrifice at your hands for the praise and glory of his name, for our good, and the good of all his Church.	Psm 50:23
WE STAND UP	
PRAYER OVER THE GIFTS	Text related to the readings of the Day
This prayer, said by the priest, is different in each single mass. When he finish we answer: **Amen.**	
PREFACE AND EUCHARISTIC PRAYER	II Cor 1:2
The Lord be with you.	Lam 3:41
And also with you.	Col 3:17
Lift up your hearts.	Col 1:3
We lift them up to the Lord.	

Let us give thanks to the Lord our God.	Mk 11:9-10
It's right to give him thanks and praise.	
Father, it is our duty and our salvation ...	
... And so, we join the angels and the saints in	
proclaiming your glory as we sing (say):	II Mac 14:36
Holy, holy, holy Lord. God of power and might.	
Heaven and earth are full of your glory. Hosanna in	
the highest. Blessed is he who comes in the name of	
the Lord. Hosanna in the highest.	
WE KNEEL	Phil 2:8 Jn 10:17-18
Lord, you are holy indeed, the fountain of all holiness.	
Let your Spirit come upon these gifts to make them holy,	Mk 14:22-25 Mt 14:22-25
so that they may become for us the body and blood of our	Lk 22:19-20.
Lord, Jesus Christ.	I Cor 11:23-25
Before he was given up to death, a death he freely	
accepted, he took bread and gave you thanks. He broke	Acts 2:23-24/I Cor 15, 3-4
the bread, gave it to his disciples, and said:	Rev 22:17 22:20
Take this, all of you, and eat it: this is my Body which will	
be given up for you.	Jn 6:51
When supper was ended, he took the cup. Again, he gave	
you thanks and praise, gave the cup to his disciples, and	I Cor 10:17
said:	
Take this, all of you, and drink from it; this is the cup of	Eph 6:18
my Blood, the Blood of the New and Everlasting	
Covenant. It will be shed for you and for all men so that	II Mac 12:45-46
sins may be forgiven.	I Cor 15, 20-23. 29-30
Do this in memory of me.	
Let us proclaim the mystery of faith.	2 Tes 1:4-5.
	Rev 7:9-15
	Heb 9:15
	I Cor 12:12-13
	Rev 7:12

Christ has died, Christ has risen, Christ will come again.
WE STAND UP
In memory of his death and resurrection,
we offer you, Father, this life-giving bread, this saving cup.
....
...Through him, with him, in him, in the unity of the
Holy Spirit, all glory and honour is yours, almighty
Father,
for ever and ever.
Amen.

RITE OF COMMUNION	Mt. 6:9-13

Let us pray with confidence to the Father in the words our Saviour gave us:

OUR FATHER

Deliver us, Lord, from every evil, and grant us peace in our day. In your mercy keep us free from sin and protect us from all anxiety as we wait in joyful hope for the coming of our Saviour, Jesus Christ.

For the kingdom, the power, and the glory are yours, now and forever.

Lord Jesus Christ, you said to your apostles: "I leave you peace, my peace I give you", look not on our sins, but on the faith of your Church, and grant us the peace and unity of your kingdom where you live for ever and ever. Jn 17:15

Amen.

The peace of the Lord be with you always.
And also with you.
**WE GIVE EACH OTHER A SIGN OF
PEACE**   Jn 14:27

**Lamb of God, you take away the sins of the world,
have mercy on us.
Lamb of God, you take away the sins of the world,
have mercy on us.
Lamb of God, you take away the sins of the world,
grant us peace.**   Jn 20.19

This is the Lamb of God who takes away the sins of the
world. Happy are those who are called to his supper.

**Lord, I am not worthy to receive you,
but only say the word and I shall be healed.** WE GO
TO RECEIVE COMMUNION   Rom 16:16

At the moment of communion, the priest or the minister
will say: **The body of Christ.**   Jn 1:29
We must answer: **Amen.**

WE RETURN TO OUR PLACE AND WE TAKE A
SIT TO PRAY QUIETLY

WE STAND UP

PRAYER AFTER COMMUNION   Rev 19:9
This prayer, said by the priest, is different in each single
mass. When he finish we answer: **Amen**
                                                            Mat 8:8

CONCLUDING RITE

The Lord be with you. **And also with you.**	**Lk 24:51**
May almighty God bless you, the Father, and the Son, and the Holy Spirit.	**Lk 7:50**
Amen. Go in the peace of Christ. **Thanks, be to God.**	**II Cor 9:15**

Printed in Great Britain
by Amazon